Moths

By Cameron Macintosh

Look at all the moths!

Moths can be little,
but some moths are big.

A moth flaps its wings!

This big moth flaps
to a lamp.

This is a moth grub.

Grubs munch and munch
to get big!

Then, the moth grub
gets in a pod.

It exits the pod as a moth.

Moths can smell very well.

And moths see well
when it's dim.

Grubs can munch,
but moths can not munch.

Moths can sip
and suck things up.

This moth sips.

This moth sucks up sap.

See the moths flap and flap!

CHECKING FOR MEANING

1. How does a moth move about? *(Literal)*

2. What do grubs do to grow bigger? *(Literal)*

3. How do grubs stay safe as they grow into moths? *(Inferential)*

EXTENDING VOCABULARY

wings	What things do you know that have *wings*? E.g. moths, birds, planes. What are these wings used for?
moth	What sound is at the end of this word? Make a list of other words you know that end in *–th*.
munch	What does *munch* mean? What are the sounds in this word? What words do you know that rhyme with *munch*?

MOVING BEYOND THE TEXT

1. What are butterflies? Are they the same as moths?

2. Find out about the life cycle of a moth. What are the stages?

3. Smell and sight are two of our senses. What are the other three?

4. Talk about why we often see moths near flowers. What are they doing?

SPEED SOUNDS

sh	ch	th	th	ck	ng
		voiced	unvoiced		

PRACTICE WORDS

wings

Moths

munch

moth

suck

things

moths